CW01511915

College Vocabulary Cartoons

Elliot Carruthers

Copyright (c) 2015
Elliot Carruthers
All Rights Reserved

ISBN-13: 978-1522965848
ISBN-10: 152296584X

Shooing away the bird
turned out to be a
pyrrhic victory.

Pyrrhic

Say: peer-rik

A victory that is too costly to the victor.

Peanut butter and jelly
makes a congruent
sandwich.

congruent

Say: kon-grew-ent

Having harmony and being compatible.

The pernicious rabbit
enjoyed the carrots in
my garden.

pernicious

Say: per-nish-ish

Something harmful usually in a gradual way.

The pedantic artist made
each brushstroke perfectly.

pedantic

Say: ped-dant-tik

Doing something in an exact or precise way.

The woman had a
penchant for wearing
flowers.

penchant

Say: pen-shant

A habitual fondess or liking of something.

He combed each hair
with meticulous care.

meticulous

Say: met-tik-you-lis

Doing something in an exact or precise way.

I like the guise of a vampire but this is not a costume party.

guise

Say: gize

Having the look or appearance of something else.

Don't worry little spider. I am not a callous person. You are safe.

callous

Say: cowl-lus

Being cruel and uncaring to others.

prepossessing

Say:
pre-poh-ses-ing

Something that is attractive to look at.

The venturesome woman smiled and jumped out of the plane.

venturesome

Say: ven-chur-sum

Willing to take on risk or danger.

The author sat unflagging until his novel was done.

unflagging

Say:
uhn-flahg-ging

Doing something in a tireless and persistent way.

It may look like bollix
but it really is a man
and his dog.

bollix

Say: bahl-liks

To mess something up or make a mistake.

wonky

Say: won-kee

Something that sits crooked or askew.

He was inconspicuous and no one realized he was there.

inconspicuous

Say:
in-kon-spik-you-us

Not easy to see or being hard to notice.

A ponderous flower
stood in the front yard.
It was huge.

ponderous

Say: pon-dur-rus

Something big, slow or awkward because of great size.

His ears were his
most predominant
feature.

predominant

Say:
pree-dahm-in-nant

The strongest or most outstanding feature of something.

There is a chasm between us. We have to agree to disagree.

chasm

Say: chaz-ihm

A divide or difference between two points.

His answers might be
dubious because he is a dog.

dubious

Say: dew-be-us

Something that is uncertain or unclear.

I understand a coat hook is utilitarian but everyone is staring at us.

utilitarian

Say:
you-til-lit-tare-re-an

Something designed
to be useful rather
than beautiful.

I did not bilk you. I told you the shirt would shrink after washing.

bilk

Say: bilk

To steal or cheat by using deception.

Maybe you should let him finish his speech before you censure him.

censure

Say: sen-shore

To condemn or
attack someone for
something they said
or did.

This photo did vindicate you.
I know you did not steal the
fish.

vindicate

Say: vin-dah-kayte

To clear someone of guilt and free them from suspicion.

He liked to flout the rules.

flout

Say: flouwt

To have contempt
for a law or to
disregard a
a rule.

Her circumlocution left them
dazed and dizzy.

circumlocution

Say

sir-kom-lo-kew-shun

Using too many words where few words are needed.

The dog could engender
good feelings in the woman.

engender

Say: en-jen-der

To create or promote feelings in someone.

The cat liked to commandeer the dog food.

commandeer

Say: Kom-man-dear

To take control of something by force.

A furtive look made him realize he forgot to wear his tie.

furtive

Say: fir-tiv

Giving a secret glance to avoid getting in trouble.

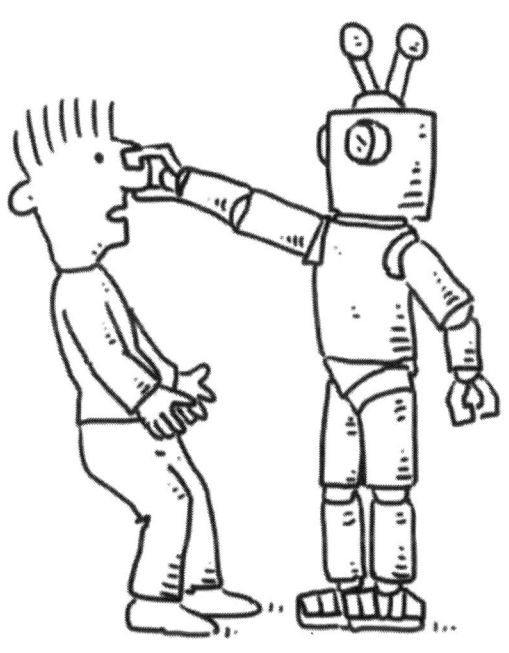

The robot was autonomous and would not listen to his commands.

autonomous

Say:
aw-tohn-no-mus

Something that has self-ruling control and the freedom to make decisions.

You did arrogate my hat.
It does not fit you.

arrogate

Say: ahr-row-gayte

To take something without permission.

The boy came to a circuitous point in the road.

circuitous

Say: sir-kew-it-tis

A route that is indirect because it is winding or curvy.

usurp

Say: you-serp

To take power by force or illegal means.

I am a dilettante but
I like painting.

dilettante

Say: dil-lah-tant

Some who does something but never becomes an expert.

predatory

Say: pread-ah-tor-ree

To take advantage of another or to exploit another.

Whoah!

The unfettered lizards
jumped all over the man.

unfettered

Say: uhn-fet-urd

To be free to roam or unchained and loose.

gallivant

Say: gal-lah-vant

To go from place to place to place in search of pleasure.

I don't understand what is so whimsical? What is so funny?

whimsical

Say: wim-sik-kal

Something funny or amusing in a charming way.

I want to talk to you
about your instructions.
They are not verbose.

verbose

Say: ver-bowse

Saying something in more words than usual.

I won't belabor the point
and I will go on my way.

belabor

Say: bee-lay-bur

To explain something repeatedly to the point of boredom.

The inimical bees were all over me. It was time to run.

inimical

Say: in-nym-ick-kal

Being hostile and unfriendly.

You dropped your money
sir. I admit my rectitde is
because of the camera.

rectitude

Say: rek-tah-tood

Having moral goodness and honesty.

Have you noticed the new
CEO is a bit callow?

callow

Say: kal-lo

Being young and inexperienced.

Here are my instructions.
It is a finite list.

finite

Say: fih-nyte

Limited in length or size.

I'd like to introduce you to
our new president of sales.
He is a potentate.

potentate

Say: poh-ten-tayte

Someone who is a kind ruler.

I have a reproof of your report. Please have a reply in the morning.

reproof

Say: ree-prooph

Showing criticism or disapproval.

I will introduce you.
Try to be less
sardonic.

sardonic

Say: sar-don-nik

Mocking someone or being sarcastic .

I think your sweater is risible. It's interesting to say the least.

risible

Say: riz-ah-bul

Something that is funny or laughable.

It was a great to juxtapose them. I can see the clown painting is better.

juxtapose

Say: juks-tah-poze

Putting two things side by side to compare them.

The tortuous hose made
watering the lawn
impossible.

tortuous

Say: tor-chew-us

Something that is twisty or windy.

The tower stood
salient. It was the
biggest thing
around.

salient

Say: Sahl-lee-ent

The most important or remarkable thing that can be seen.

The end.

30559611R00057

Printed in Great Britain
by Amazon